*a collection of prose and poetry
on the theme of friendship*

for

a

friend

LUCENT DREAMING

First Edition

For a Friend
Published by Lucent Dreaming Ltd.
103 Bute Street, Cardiff, CF10 5AD

Copyright © 2024 Multiple Authors.
The moral right of the authors has been asserted.
All rights reserved. Printed in the United Kingdom by 4edge Ltd.
No part of this book may be reproduced without written permission
from the authors.

Copyright © 2024 Cover artwork by Amy Moody.
Edited by Samiha Meah & Lisa Kay Byus.

ISBN 978-1-916632-11-0

Lucent Dreaming acknowledges the financial support of
Books Council of Wales and Creative Wales.

CYNGOR LLYFRAU CYMRU
BOOKS COUNCIL of WALES

Contents

Introduction *Samiha Meah & Lisa Kay Byus*	5
How To Write A Poem For A Friend *Jane Burn*	7
Advice-Poem *Olivia Walwyn*	10
What We Telepath When We Telepath About Love *Marie Vibbert*	12
chosen kin tapestry *Ell Huang*	19
A Butterfly Fell on my Head *Yana Fay Dzedze*	22
For Carolann *Sarah Terkaoui*	24
For Lewis *Briony Collins*	26
Ruth's Poem *Ella Sadie Guthrie*	28
dear Nyxïa *Sodïq Oyèkànmí*	30

For Lauren On A Tuesday *Chloe McIntosh*	31
Elegy *Melissa Joplin Higley*	33
Observed *Angela Townsend*	34
Love Songs *Daisy Edwards*	37
Art Dates with my Best Friend *Mabel Ros*	39
Read 3:14 AM *Maggie D'Isa-Hogan*	44
The Visitor *Elodie A. Roy*	46
Your Door *Lynne Sargent*	49
To The Ones Greyed By The Blue-Stringed Ventriloquist *Neethu Krishnan*	51
Self-Love *Tom Mallouk*	54
With all the news for what ensues, I choose to hope and believe. *Jordan Zuniga*	55

The Sky and the Sky and the Sky *Steve Denehan*	57
The Sweetest Tough Cookie *B. Anne Adriaens*	59
To Braid a Cable *Chloe Orrock*	60
Odysseus Wants To Hear About My School Play *Rachel Bruce*	61
This Grimoire Belongs to Miss Cleo Jackson *Elis Montgomery*	63
Not Half Jar of Peanut Butter *Colette Tennant*	73
A letter to a friend about scrambled eggs *Jon Chan*	74
Spaghetti Bridge *Izzy Searle*	76
Will Oceans Converge in Our Village Park? *Alex Harford*	78
10 Names of Happiness *Taher Adel*	82
Author biographies	87

For a friend

Introduction

Samiha Meah & Lisa Kay Byus

Beyond our familial relationships, friendships are perhaps the most fundamental and fulfilling connections we can have as humans. They are our first point of contact when we step out into the wider world as children and then, again, as adults. Friends will hold you up and stumble alongside you through every awkward phase, every heartbreak and every moment of joy. It is comfortable and easy – another home to come back to when the world feels unfamiliar and strange.

    When compiling the pieces for this anthology, we wanted to showcase stories and poems that captured the unique beauty of friendship, in all its multitudes, in its highs and lows, in its most perfect moments and in its most enduring. Friendship is a gift, and this anthology, a gift to friends.

    From poems dedicated to friends who live vividly in

memories to tales of childhood friendships that deepen and strengthen with age; in the overreaching happiness we wish to extend to those we love and the moments that exist in between; to friendship in its simplest form and in its most complex. The works of these writers are snapshots of the different ways friendship can take shape and move us. It is a reminder to us that we are never truly alone and that there is always a shoulder to lean on.

Our connections to those around us are more important than ever. To the friendships we have forged over many years and to the ones still beginning: Thank you. To our contributors, thank you for sharing your words and your friends with us. And to the friends of Lucent Dreaming, who have been here every step of the way: Thank you. You make this possible.

How To Write A Poem
For A Friend

Jane Burn

At first, you may not know exactly where to begin.
How do you decide which friend the poem will be for?
Your best friend? A childhood friend?
One who has remained, forever loyal by your side?
A penfriend? You only meet through letters,
but their words mean everything.

A friend from work, a good neighbour,
the fur or feathers kind? A college friend? One you met
in the worst or the happiest of times? Friend in need
or fair-weather friend? One who believes in you –
who says *reach for the sky!* One who keeps your feet
upon the ground, who always tells you the absolute truth?

A friend who is no longer with you? Friend estranged?
Friend reunited? Imaginary friend? A friend you made
on holiday? An almost-happened friend – someone
you talked to in the supermarket, on the train,
during the interval of a play, or bought
a second-hand table from – you sensed a kindred spirit

and thought of the saying, *strangers are only friends
who haven't met*. Making friends takes courage – sometimes
it doesn't happen even though you wish it had. Maybe
you want to write a poem for a friend who is beyond
your reach. Perhaps your friend is a garden – a place
to remember or be remembered. An old stuffed bear,

who has listened to every secret told, worn threadbare
inside your embrace? What if the greatest friend
you have is yourself? Write a poem to your bones,
your mind, your skin, your breath. Imagine this friend
as the dawn – turn their friendship into the sunrise,
into the sound of morning birds. Tell them about a dream

you had – the one where the stars became philosophers,
where your glasses turned into owls and flew away
from your head. Imagine the way your friend completely
understands. Make a sonnet where the volta turns
from dream, to real, to love. Imagine your friendship
as a horse. Its gallop is the two of you, meeting again

after travelling many miles. Its wise eye
is your friend's counsel. Its heart is eighteen times larger
than a human one. And that is your friend's heart.
It keeps the whole of their life inside and still has room
for you. Imagine your friendship as a forest –
how sometimes it's a weight of leaves, sometimes

a weight of snow. How trees have their own way
of speaking, how deep the roots go. Make them a poem
built from friendship – each word two syllables, the same.
Picnic, pencil, catnap, ballroom, cobweb, winter, happy.
Try words that rhyme with friend. Mend, send, lend, depend.
Try synonyms – companion, ally, confidante. Make a poem

that says *I'm here, any time you need, as you have always
been for me*. Make a poem about the journeys you have taken
together. Find ten similes to describe the way they laugh.
Imagine your friend as a castle – strong and safe, built to last.
Imagine them close, even if you must be far apart.
Imagine them a home inside your heart.

Друг, vän, caraid, přítel, saaxiib, bandhu. Frënd.

Advice-Poem

Olivia Walwyn

Start with right where you are.
Look. Listen.
Ask what it is you want to keep.
What it is you want to pass on to your children.

Filter these essentials
from the sea of surface data, through your feelings,
observing
how they sway and flex
like a fisherman's net. Take only what you need.

Travel light. Put one foot
in front of the next. Don't sweat.
Become acquainted with the boundary
of your own skin.

Inhabit your body.
Feel the wind. Observe the way one thing
follows the next. The flight of birds.
Flowers. Leave minimal tracks.

Observe the way things grow
at the side of the pavement. Views opening
in the most unlikely, decimated of places.

Listen to your daughter's breath.

Listen to the air reverberate
with the scar of a long-haul flight.

Watch its gradual heal across the sky.
Never think you've covered everything.

Go on instinct. Go on a hunch. Go because we must
have hope. Go on. Go now.

Consider the quality of the air.
Breathe as if you breathed
for the person you loved the most
in the whole world. Know these are just words.

Advice-Poem Olivia Walwyn

What We Telepath When We Telepath About Love

Marie Vibbert

It's Tuesday and I've stacked the dirty supper plates but I'm taking a moment before washing, admiring the tin table I inherited from Dad, rubbing the nail-polish-painted depression where I cracked the enamel with a meat mallet when I was ten. Time rewards small villainies.

I reach out and find your mind open. You're reading your kids a bedtime story. That one with the duck in a raincoat. You are sitting on the edge of Jess' bed, your left butt cheek tight from maintaining your perch. I feel the flannel blanket dragging against your jeans, smell the dirty clothes and baby-sweat.

Through the archway that separates my kitchen and dining room I see Rae at his desk – really an old television cabinet crammed between the baker's rack and the window. Rae is supposed to be doing something for his job, but he keeps opening cat videos. He knows he's procrastinating and feels guilty, but he always gets the work done at bedtime in a mad fit of self-punishment.

My love for him mixes with exasperation, salt and sweet. I want to kiss his slack lips while his eyes dart like the cats he admires.

In your house across town, on that clinging flannel bedspread, you cringe. Thoughts of love are hard between us, and I lingered on that one. I'm usually better about not dwelling on Rae when we're connected.

For a friend

You recall the time you heard Rae wish he wasn't married. It pops up reflexively, wanting to hurt me back. I recognize in the shape of your attack the narrow, deep wound left by the love you had for your ex.

That's not it, you insist, and your anger interrupts the flow of bedtime story, your voice stalls. Your son's forehead squinches up in that old-man seriousness children can summon like a knife to the heart.

But I'm right. You ache for your ex, that feverish absorption when you first met, how he looked at you like he could use the curve of your hips to unlock the secrets of the universe. I politely don't mention the misery of overhearing your thoughts when you were like two halves of a magnet.

But of course, you feel me deciding not to, and judge me for it. You recall your passion as greater and easier than mine for Rae. You think I'm bitter at the comparison.

My memory is different. You had your doubts about your husband from the start; his emotional baggage a foreign design to our well-known packs and trunks. I told you to talk to him about it. You said it was hard to bring up unspoken things when telepaths aren't supposed to exist.

His three younger sisters entitled him to always be right, to have all these images of proper feeding and diapering and exactly how to powder, but you couldn't complain when he swallowed his objections and kept his face patient.

How to begin to describe the gulf of experience between our tight we-two-ness and his loosely organized army of cousins? His idea of family was a jumble of toys in a box; ours one puzzle with many interlocking pieces.

Your anger mellows into admiring the finer points of

your grief. It took years for the intensity of your thirst for each other to boil off, leaving you as co-workers in the job of raising two kids, amicable co-workers at first, and then indifferent, and then hostile.

It's now three years and seven months after the divorce. I check my math on a scrap of receipt. Almost eight months.

But wasn't it lovely? You muse. The thrills of anticipation and release, like you had a beautiful secret you could only express on each other's skin.

I need to get moving on these dishes. I stand to fill the sink. You close your book and gently argue the kids into staying put while you tuck the covers around them. I let the first plate tip like a sinking boat into the hot, soapy water.

You think that there's this purposeful wall in my head, blocking off everything bad about my partner while I hypocritically assert how true and honest my quieter love is than your doomed passion.

Maybe when we say love is blind, that's what we mean? I see his flaws; I don't care about them. I let them sink from sight, like this cup under the foam of dish-soap.

Rae dated awful people, both men and women. Eyes wide open, he fell into the trap again and again, a promise of warmth and security, turned into jealousy and fists. What did it say about him, that he thought that was love? What did it say about me, that I was the one he stayed with?

I was the honest version of what he'd yearned for. He admires my strength, my willingness to speak to managers and say no to solicitors for him. I'm so macho I can wash dishes on a weeknight in a pink frilly apron. I shake my hips to make the ruffle flutter. I love this stupid apron. It makes me feel like a movie star from the fifties as I swipe my rag around inside the stew pot.

You call it cosplay. I only do the dishes when Rae's quarterly reports are due. You remember how I screamed like I was being burned when our mother would try to wrestle me into a dress. You would already be in its mate, demurely brushing out creases.

I marvel at the length of the journey I took, to forgive pink.

I set the last pot in the rack and pour myself a shot of gin with my still-soapy hands.

Your heart just broke: a tiny, regulated, daily break, as you give yourself one last gaze at the children before stepping into the hall. They're not asleep yet, but earnestly and obediently pretending, and you are enjoying the moment, acknowledging that part of the pleasure is the silence, that your kids are not badgering you for anything, and won't for the next eight hours, if you're lucky.

My heart squeezes that I get to share this.

I resume my seat at the table with gin in hand, thinking about quiet love. The love of exchanging chores. Like my wanting Rae not to wound himself with a late night. He makes me a better person because of his flaws.

If I were to choose something to recall fondly of your ex, it would be when he explained to you how and when to use fabric softener, not because he expected you to take the chore over, but because he was excited to have figured it all out, and your heart swelled.

You're walking very carefully to your kitchen. You draw out a chair and pour yourself a glass of wine. Chianti, yuck. I experience your gratification at the scent, anticipating the dryness and complexity that you love, and I will feel as love, but mingled with the seasick memories of my own reaction to those flavors.

Better than the burn of gin, you think. But you also savor the hit of addiction-fulfillment that comes when I hold the glass rim against my lips and inhale. I always picture walking through a wintery forest, the comingled memories of past satisfactions that flavors and sometimes covers the first sip entirely.

We enjoy enjoying, reflected and separate.

Memories of the painful, hurtful years come up. High School. Competition. Not wanting to be "one of the twins". That was me. I pursued popularity at any price, only to discover, much later, of course, that the purchase price of popularity is to be content in oneself. The lack of want buffets the self-esteem of popular kids like an excellent skincare routine.

Stupid of a mind-reader. I didn't care enough about their inner worlds, too caught up in my own. I'd drowned a fellow lifeboat survivor in the hopes of being picked up by an anti-drowning league.

The metaphor needs work. You laugh and imagine me drowning in Chianti, but you forgive me one smidge more. You are fond of my metaphor-making. It feels exactly like my fondness for Rae's cat videos.

My mind wanders to the first cup of coffee waiting for me tomorrow morning. The machine is right there, stained and finger-printed, an almost living potential. I'll fill the reservoir and the filter before bed.

Rae stretches. He is reaching the point where he'll close the videos and actually work. He is rising to physically separate the two phases of computer-use.

You dislike the texture of his cheeks, the sags under his eyes. I don't like the evidence of age, no, the inevitable end of our time together creeping closer, but he is still handsome, even when he's been staring at a monitor for hours.

You suspect my eyesight is failing.

Rae grips my bicep briefly in passing, and he drops a brief kiss on the nape of my neck that sends a thrill down my spine. He gets a glass and fills it at the sink.

Say what you will about his tired eyes, his rear end looks perfect in those sweatpants.

Now this is a repeat offense on my part, back to the beginning of the argument, when we had been making such progress. Why must I keep inflicting him on you?

Hormones, I guess. I offer to listen to you taste any number of glasses of Chianti.

You want a thrill down your spine now and then.

It has nothing on tonight's last glance at your kids, at their dear eyelashes against their full, soft cheeks.

You don't want to agree. You want to be purely, completely bereft. But their eyelashes were, indeed, so cute.

The gin is making my brain warm caramel. The wine is doing the same for you. Lightweight.

Lush, you counter.

I feel the children's minds growing slow and heavy with sleep, and I feel Rae focused on numbers, and I feel you slowly unspooling from the fear of a thousand disasters that could befall two school-age kids on a Tuesday. But it's always like that. You always worry. You worry about me.

We unpack our worries together and turn them into

comfort. You'll go to bed and dream of your ex, though you hope you won't, and I'll dream of fuel injectors, because my job is seeping into my subconscious mind, but that's okay.

We should get on with these things, but we won't. We sit at our respective kitchen tables with our drinks, open but not thinking. There's always another burden to share, like a thick, warm blanket.

chosen kin tapestry

Ell Huang

so much depends on
mischief like ours:
futures & pasts, tethers &
threads we'd imagined,
stringing us together from
long ago, before
we knew each other's
voices, faces, names.

where we were not blood,
invisible strings just *maybe*
tied us together, fated to meet.

you were the brother I never had.
arm in arm, you taught me the Viking's grip,
a spontaneous transfer of energy.
and, even if too quickly, all at once,
we stitched ourselves together
a tapestry of vibrant, distressed rug
until our lives, vastly different as they were,
were sewn together, our flag colors unfurled
side by side; and in the far-flung
future, we still had each other's numbers,
memories, remnants of souls, destinies.

in these dreams, in so many ways,
I'd meet your husband. an invitation
inked and stamped with royal seal,
because you were never one to hold back
from fancy. Me, loving a fantasy made real,
I'd attend. You had no choice but to invite me,
you'd say, as if wary of a dark fairy's power.
I'd watch as you'd crown each other's heads
before a kiss. I'd be there to celebrate.

and other ways, too. perhaps in
a European marketplace, your name
scattered and known among the
sleepy, smiling bakers and tavern keepers.
a cobblestone journey, a house with an observatory,
a bearded husband who studies stars, and a child
with a gecko on her head, reptile now full grown.
I read your books to her, you'd admit to me.

a gala a decade into the future, corona long past.
your husband dragging you back to America
after a backpacking trip in the mountains.
a clamoring party much to your fancy,
and many men you've kissed and introduced.
and then, a sight across the room, you bend your head over
and in awe, see me. director, screenwriter, bestselling author,
we would've made it then, you say, & in the vision,
we reunite, recounting the olden apocalypse days
we thought we'd never survive, but did.
in this enchanted party, drinks flowing to the brim,
with platonic declaration of love, you'd be there to celebrate.

and even as a joke, I'd send you a wedding invitation.
you'd scratch your head and turn to your husband(s)
wondering what could have happened to me,
your asexual, aromantic counterpart
whose love was not much for any exchange of rings.
it'd be up to you, then, what to do with this information.
what imposter there must be! what murder mystery!
what strange plot twist. your intrigue, having bonded with me
having tied together and made spirits kin,
would be too strong. you'd have to know if it's really me.
you'd attend, if only to investigate.

in this possible future, wouldn't it be funny
if our two threads of fate wound differently
in this great oriental carpet tapestry, and finally
in this picture, meet again, gathered into tassels
at the end? I'm not one for believing in soulmates

anymore, because we weren't made
to twine together forever or even complement.
But maybe we're still woven in the same tapestry,
an interstellar one, and in that,
We're kin. We're made.

A Butterfly Fell on my Head

Yana Fay Dzedze

A butterfly fell on my head today. I thought of you. At first, I was sure it was a leaf that patted my hair before it tumbled to the grass, but I looked down to see a ruffled little orange thing catching its wings before flying away. We were in a peaceful place. My daughter rolled on her colourful blanket, and together we gazed at the green leaves above. A big dog with friendly eyes lolloped over to say hello, sagging grey ears pulled to the floor by aged curiosity. A kaleidoscope of butterflies flittered against a blue sky, wings beating a silent magic into the air, and I continued to wonder what words I might gift you.

I've been waiting for a story to fall upon my head the way the butterfly did. A breeze rustled the bendy branches of the trees and I continued to gaze at the orange wings, glimmering. There was once a time when each of those butterflies danced as a possibility in the infinite, not yet alive. I love the mystery of that non-existent space that we all come from.

There is an absurdity that sits at the heart of that mystery. A deep knowing of the things we are unable to grasp. Like the becoming of a butterfly or the birth of our children. The curiosity forever pulls at us, and we become Alice, tumbling through a rabbit hole into warped worlds subject to nature's whims.

It's scary to not have control. To be a creature on earth, born from the inexplicable nothingness. To be a crawling caterpillar human, dragging yourself through reality to find food to chomp and shelter to nestle into. Survival is a gravity: it presses us to look at life without escape. Wraps us in a straight-jacket, a people-pupa that we liquidate within, to grow our own wings. We must all face the sacred struggle of breaking free into a life where we can defy gravity and dance against cloud-speckled skies.

    I realise now that there is no story waiting to fall upon my head. Very simply, a message to you: Breathe. All the way into what is happening in your world. The coming apart and falling together of all that is wrong and right, is perfection. The chaotic barefoot wild-garden kind of perfection, void of neat lines or control. Return to the knowing within, that there are no mistakes, only endless opportunities to meet this tremendous world and the gentle exquisiteness of your own existence. Your presence matters; there is nothing for you to do other than what your heart most desires. Fall down the rabbit hole as many times as you wish. Perhaps once is enough for now, but who knows? Maybe you'll get a taste for the thrill of your own greatness, armed with the knowing that emotions are fleeting and all of this, the burden—and the blessing—will pass. Do not ask the rain to fall another day. Do not attempt to manipulate the sun to shine when it hides behind the clouds. Let nature move in all its wisdom—in the world around you, and within you too. In ways deeper than any human mind can comprehend, you are loved, you are held, you are barefoot wild-garden perfection. Fly.

For Carolann

Sarah Terkaoui

I'll meet you by the dogwood
that finds itself in the flames
of your hair. You will be as ever
kind and clever and curious.

Shahrazad. Isotta Nogarola.
Gertrude Bell. Life swollen full,
epic soaked. Your toes lightly
mapped the earth. North and south,

east and west, collecting language
and lovers, books and beloveds
music and its makers in your summertime,
decades moving lightly through open hands

scattering their seeds as you passed by.
Flowers bloom where you left your life's libretto,
poppies, cornflowers and buttercups,
around and beneath the orchard trees,

guarding the damson plums and crab apples
that saw your stardust words make worlds
of the air about us, as they escaped
your pen, your meditations, your memories,

where you were a girl once more,
riding the width of the wind, fingers tracing
moon rivers across continents, feet
debutant dancing to your fables

And me? I'm waiting for you to find me
by the dogwood, ready to catch
the tilt of your smile, ready my friend,
to walk with you once more.

For Carolann Sarah Terkaoui

For Lewis

Briony Collins

The driveway of my mind is gravel
It flies up if I move too fast

He sees my face and knows

Takes me by the crook of my arm
Leads me outside the pub to the road
Away from the music

We are green
LED beaming above the doorway
Emerald flecks in his eyes
Glass bottles swilling their elixir

We are spring adjacent
Tree cells whistling in their chlorophyll
Moss swelling between bricks
Dampening in the midnight of rooves

He sees my face and knows

Says the only colours on this road
Are hi-vis yellow and siren red
No green at all

I look at him and see spring
See leaves and moss and life
Hang myself around his neck
      and choose

Ruth's Poem
For Ruth Boon

Ella Sadie Guthrie

I want to write a poem about heartbreak,
but I don't want to be soppy about it. I've spent
too many lines comparing you to the weather.
Instead, I'm going to write a poem how Ruth would.
She would look at this and say *I knew it*. She'd say *Love
feels like a tractor churning up wet mud on cold mornings
on the kind of farms where they turn newborn baby calves
to veal*, which is to say, not very nice. She'd say something like
*Love is like sitting backwards on a southern train that's been
diverted through Littlehampton*, sometimes it makes you nauseous.
She'd be specific about it. I know what she'd say about this.
She'd say *I told you so*, but she'd say it in a disjointed and
poetic kind of way and also say that *He's a dick* and *A man
playing with your heart like a child under the age of five plays
with an old Baby Born*—which is to say not very carefully—
is not worth good dick. She'd tell me to *Stop being so romantic*
about it, stop using rose petals falling and birds chirping to translate
a feeling which is really just a chemical reaction, not too dissimilar
to the one I feel when I smoke tobacco rolled in non-branded
   Rizla paper.
Ruth smokes tobacco between her middle and ring finger, like
   the only
entity she could see herself committing to is a cigarette.
Ruth would be happy I'm getting over you. She wouldn't tell me
to write your name on a piece of paper and burn it, she doesn't believe

in witchy shit. She'd tell me to imagine you as the piece of
   paper instead
Scrunch it up and throw it against a brick wall painted off-white,
the kind of colour kids bounce half deflated footballs against at
   school.
I imagine you are the half-deflated football, and I am
   Beckham's right foot,
just the right one, and I kick you against the wall until all the
nitrogen
mixed with oxygen is gone and I've suffocated it to death.

dear Nyxïa

Sodïq Oyèkànmí

        permit me to start again. & maybe this time we can start afresh from a distinct margin. i/ too understand the morphology of being. that a body is nothing but a *body* if the mind & soul fled the space.
you said you felt so small this morning. *some weird fragmentation going on in the home of my body.* your body laden with grief. with dreams [yet unlocked]. with fear. with —
fear nothing/ those grey skies are but God's own orchestra assembling to sing your name.   fear nothing/
the mouth of the day is not wide open to devour you but to usher you into its glorious light.   fear nothing/
the night is not here to sour the sweetness nestled on the sill of your brown eyes.   fear nothing/
i'm here to let you know you are safe in your body. you are safe. in your body. you are safe —
so comrade. march/ brave & beautiful with your lucent laughter straight into the arms of the world.

For Lauren on a Tuesday

Chloe McIntosh

So, you've never met a dog you didn't like
And I've never met a person quite like you

Radiant and warm,
Righteous like a Libra

Every thought of you is fire ember, amber sky,
Russet hearted girl

Space age sick and fierce

To watch you sprout and grow
Into the person you always were
Beneath it all,
The rage and uncertainty
The summer sadness and the Cornish castle

Makes me feel maturity like nothing else

Level-headed, sure-footed,
Quick-witted,
Kismet met
Abundance

Like autumn leaves forever,
You just keep coming
And rustling my life

So, maybe we will have that observatory-cum-lighthouse
Where we raise our babies named after fierce girls
From fateful books

Or maybe you'll keep chasing space
All over the world
And I'll keep writing poetry to fill the absences
That never cease

But there will always be good murder mysteries to read
And favourite pop songs to sing in the car

I can't promise that you'll be in my life forever
But I'd like it very much if you were

After all,
There's a new mac and cheese recipe to try out
A neighbour's puppy to say hello to

And there will always be a full bottle of rum
In my cupboard
Reserved just for you

Elegy
For Jill

Melissa Joplin Higley

If we had known—two teenaged girls
in the summer of '88, driving barefoot
at midnight through the pine barrens
of the Atlantic coastal plain, blanket
pallet in the hatch—if we had known
that you had only fifteen more years—
if we had known that, at thirty-two,
the same cancer would breed
in our breasts—if we had known that I,
the lucky one, would be beside your bed,
holding your hand; that your fingers
would stiffen no matter how much
I massaged; that the clear polish applied
to your cooling fingertips would reveal
the purple-gray of your weakening heart;
that the pulse would fade first
from your feet, then from your hands;
that I would speak our stories, our
goodbyes, while you could only blink tears
through morphine; that I would miss
your final breath—if we had known—
two teenaged girls in the summer of '88,
racing each other down the moonlit beach,
wet sand flying from our swift, bare feet—
what else would we have done? Despite
the dark water, the indifferent surf,
side-by-side, in we dove.

Observed

Angela Townsend

We pay attention because we cherish, but there is no telling which comes first.

In sixteen years working at the cat sanctuary, I have loved nearly four thousand whiskered aliens. Sure, many of them have perfectly round eyes. But only Betsy, the cat who knows my secrets, could capture me in those apples. I was dabbing on my deodorant — a moment when someone is attuned to wonder — when I absently look over and see her, all sea-glass and searching. Engulfed in love for the cat who is my own, I notice her eyes are a more perfect circle than the earth itself. Holy moly. (I believe these were my actual and out-loud words.) I notice, and I adore.

We pay attention because we cherish, but love is not too proud to wear dungarees daily.

Mail carriers dot the world like ladybugs, thousands of stories on strong legs. Surely, all of them are exceptional, beloveds in blue. But only my mailman, shy string bean in a mustache, holds my *Taste of Home* magazines and tax documents like newborns. In six years, he has never not been startled by my presence. He has never not smiled, bushy and bashful. He has never not cradled his duty like an offering. I see him loping, long-legged through the neighborhood and he reminds me of my uncle, and everyone's uncle, and my trust in the alphabet of the ordinary. I notice him, and I love the letters that write us all over the walls of each other's boxes.

We pay attention because we cherish, but affection has

the authority to overtake us unawares.

There are no fewer than six supermarkets within a close radius of my condo. Surely, all of them shine with helpful employees and polished pears and boggling selections of plant-based provolone. But only my Giant, the smallish one, has Gabe. I have a friend in the self-checkout, a legend in a red apron with a pompadour that only makes sense on his particular head. He coos to befuddled shoppers, "You got this, Jack. Mm-hmm, green button. YEAH! Aw-RIGHT!" They check back in. The world is as cool as the grey-haired greaser who believes in everyone. He's funny because he's unhinged. He's lovable because life has no hinges.

You may caution my exuberance here at the automatic doors. If everything can be cherished, doesn't the word lose meaning? Should we not preserve our tenderness for the sweetest fruit? Must we dilute the scraggly word "love" by slathering it on the supermarket?

I will slather with abandon. If love is the law of the universe, nothing is beyond its fingertips. Fondness for one supermarket just might lead to love for one neighbor. Love, inefficient and alive, is about the one.

We pay attention because we cherish, but love always gives back too much change, then runs down the hall giggling. The more I notice, the more I am seized with affection in all directions. The condition is progressive.

I realize my boss wears electric blue or safety orange on gloomy days. I see my neighbor take in her ceramic dogs and angels when it rains. I hear the radio DJ mean every word of "Have a bangin' day!" I glimpse the sweat behind the poem by the blogger with four readers. I catch the kindness in the kitchen that concocted low-carb waffles.

We pay attention because we cherish, and if we're willing to pay the price, we are in very real peril of loving everywhere.

Love Songs

Daisy Edwards

They don't write love songs about
cry-laughing during a D&D game
because your friend
genuinely thought introducing
Capitalism
to a *fish*
would help them spy on the bad guys.
The way my diaphragm choked me,
how I couldn't see for the tears
and my voice shook from giggling
doesn't feature in a single verse.
Neither does crowding round a too-small coffee table
that is host to an over-the-top cheese board
because that is how they do it here.
After feasting, we play board games and talk through films.
The only reason I drift off is from weariness, I promise, because
this kind of joy bubbles up and out of me.
They need to write songs about how
we are all so busy and tired
and burning at both ends
while trying to make those same ends meet,
and how in the group chat we exchange:
Emojis   Advice   Photos   Complaints
They are in my pocket and I am in theirs.
There are no love songs written about this;
about how my face hurts from smiling
and how my posture relaxes and I stop looking over my shoulder,

about how a version of myself dreamed of this.
There needs to be songs about this,
if there were I would play it for you now and we would dance
 for five minutes
before collapsing on the sofa and talking about all the
 unimportant things we know.

Art Dates with my Best Friend

Mabel Ros

"Your eyes will become square," my mum used to say when I stared at screens for too long. I must have really wanted them that shape, I think as I sit in my studio at 8.00 am, staring at square screens, with square documents and tiny square grids. A dream job, sat at home – supermarket pyjamas as uniform. I had surrounded myself with illustrations, books, and plant cuttings on the windowsill, to remind myself of the artistic dream plan, but when working, I was just going through the grids.

The only source of light this gloomy early morning is the computer eclipsing my view. Outside, the world is overcast and even the blooming trees are plain grey. From September to March, it had all been dark. A second source of light blinks suddenly to my left. A notification indicating a voice note from Aura.

"Heey Luu, what's up? I have the day off. Bristol day?"

We weren't the kind to talk on the phone, more of paper and pen – it'd been six months since we last hung out, but I know exactly what she meant.

Ten years ago, on that first day in *English for Foreigners* class, she had seen me write *bibliothèque* in my notebook in an attempt to make my native Spanish sound English, only to end up sounding French. Our friendship had been constructed one museum, train ride, bowl of ramen and bookshop at a time.

The hangout proposal wakes me from my Excel trance. I send a voice note right back.

"There's a bus at 9.00 am, I'll be there before midday!" I send back. The countdown for departure begins at 8.09 am. One must dress up for the semiannual occasion; last year's Christmas pyjamas won't cut it, but what will? The seemingly tidy spare room quickly explodes when I open the closet door, an avalanche of clothes. By the time it hits 8.20 am, I have already sorted through several options. I decide on a long dress with a jumper only to change my mind again last minute. After frantically packing my bag and ensuring the cat is taken care of, I stumble out the door at 8.55 am. I lock the door behind me, skip the wet doormat, and rush to the bus stop. I arrive with less than one minute to spare; I message Aura while standing on a bus packed with people to tell her I am on my way.

"Where are you?" Aura messages – she has arrived at Cabot Circus, our meeting spot between the bus and train station, one minute before me. This was a crowded shopping place, even on a Thursday morning.

"I can see you," I reply. "Ahhhhh, look at you!" She always looked cool – the encounter brings some squeaks and a small dance out of me, while Aura is more contained. "Coffee," I say as we clasp our arms around each other and walk into the cheapest shop nearby.

"Two café lattes plis, two lattes," I say in my strongest Spanish accent.

"Two regular lattes to go please," Aura clarifies to the perplexed lady at the counter. "What has it been, ten years or ten days?" She jokes, but I swear I've mastered the language since then.

I feel droplets when we step outside, but as we walk with our first coffee of the day over wet cobblestones and with no route, the sun hits just right. At that moment instead of stopping for a photo, I take one with my mind.

There was a time when I walked with three cameras on hand, dragged my friends out on adventures and enjoyed dressing up. That was how this friendship started, bonding over adventure and dreams of foreign lands. There might have been talks about homesickness a while later, but the last three years, from twenty-nine to thirty-one, adventures were replaced by writings and lectures to claim some sense of being back. While I craved solitude and lived an ocean away from most, my social circle had gone quiet; so had I.

This glorious morning, we decide to walk up Park Street to the museum, to just exist around art. In between chandeliers, a replica of a Bristol Boxkite hangs from the glass ceiling in the big hall. Looking up in awe, an intrusive feeling overtakes me, wary of someone calling me out, which was quickly eased by running upstairs past the dinosaur, to the painting galleries.

"Which one is your favourite?" I ask in the Victorian room.

"I think I prefer the Renaissance and classic sculptures," Aura says looking around. "What about yours?"

"From this room, I think this one is my favourite." I point at the big *Garden Court* by Edward Burne-Jones that covers half the wall. Every time I visit, I stand in front of it and imagine being in there. Later, in the gift shop, we buy post cards of the painting to use as bookmarks, to remember today.

"Why are they all sleep? Or..." Aura looks closely at the postcard.

"It is one of a few works about Sleeping Beauty." In

retrospect, I can see how it could be perceived as a tragedy. The six sleeping women are relaxed in their poses; it was almost easy to mistake them for dead, but it brings me peace whenever I look at them.

"I quite fancy another coffee now," I say as I hold the door.

"And cake!" Aura exclaims. On our way back down Park Streets' hill, we browse the vintage shops.

"This coffee shop looks nice, and look…" I point inside. "Four-fifty for cake and a coffee." I order two coffees, a lemon drizzle and the last slice of carrot cake for her. "I don't want to jinx it, but… it looks more sunny now, should we sit outside?"

The light was now great; I snap a photo of Aura as I walk behind her. We stroll along College Green Park and find a dry spot on the corner of Deanery Road, in front of the library. Grand stone buildings, gothic windows, coffee, and cake – afternoon sun, comfortable silence, and a friend.

On our way back to the morning meeting spot, we stop by a few bookshops and share some quotes, but for the most part we browse the shelves with our minds lost.

We arrive back at our meeting spot and know it is time to part ways again. "My bus leaves in 10 minutes, I've got to go!" I say, breaking into the goodbye dance.

Aura heads towards the train station and I leave for the bus stop. With lighter shoulders I walk away in a quick sprint to catch the bus. I play some music and sit with my backpack on my lap – a few minutes later my phone lights up with a message.

"Send me the photos from today!" she wrote. I don't

have as many as usual today, but I send the one I took outside the coffee and cake place.

When I get home, I run upstairs to where the cat greets me with a yawn. The sun coming in through the window paints the studio in fiery light – it is like looking through my orange summer sunglasses. The happy hue gets into my stomach and I feel the urge to move that square screen away; this is no place for spreadsheets, but a space to create! On the windowsill, the roots of the cuttings in water are growing.

I send another message. "Thank you for sharing your peace with me today my friend, let's not wait another six months again."

Read 3:14 AM

Maggie D'Isa-Hogan

how r u doing?
we havent talked in awhile
so i thought id shoot u a quick text

im sorry about ur mom.
she always seemed happy when she picked us up from school
how r u doing?

i know im not ur best friend anymore
but im not anyone elses best friend yet
so i thought id shoot u a quick text

i dreamt my phone vanished so i tap-tap-tapped on my palm
my messages brought me to u and i held u tight
how r u doing?

I dreamt I tried to stay with you this time
but i wasnt fast enough or clever enough and i lost u in the crowd
so i thought id shoot u a quick text

i dream about u more often than we talk these days
in my dreams u smell like u did when we were kids
how r u doing?

i dont need u 2 respond
I want 2 leave a piece of myself in ur pocket 4 u 2 hold
so i thought id shoot u a quick text

i know its not enough
but only so many words can carry over so many kinds of distance.
how r u doing?
i thought id shoot u a quick text

The Visitor

Elodie A. Roy

You phoned to say you were coming. The thought of your visit keeps me happy for days. The morning before you arrive, I tidy the studio. The three windows are clean, but I feel they ought to be cleaner and bigger still, to let more of the light in. I would like the entire summer to pour into the room. I imagine the studio flat unmoored, gently bobbing away – like a frail paper boat dissolving into a pool of light. At the last moment, I hurry to the corner shop to buy cigarettes and a pack of chocolate biscuits. You're not eating much these days, yet part of me longs to feed you.

There is slowness and softness wherever you are. It shocks me every time – this infinite, hesitant slowness of yours. It surrounds you like a halo. I like watching you move your thin hands as you speak. You drink your coffee in small, absent sips. All your gestures seem suspended, unfinished – the motions one makes in a dream. What are we speaking about? What keeps us so absorbed for hours? It is odd; I never quite remember our conversations afterwards. Words vanish as we utter them. They never leave a trace. We haphazardly drift from one topic to another, smoking and speaking. Our words are like faint, drowsy signs: the names of continental cities we hardly saw and barely remember; the plays we were both in; the people we've lost. After a while nothing really matters anymore. Every word is an approximation, an excuse to stay together a bit longer. Shall I make more coffee? Would you like another biscuit? Are you going to be in Liverpool for a while? We don't see each other as often these days. I apologise for the hard, uncomfortable kitchen chairs. You stretch your long, thin legs in front of you; the chairs are fine, you don't like being too comfortable. You've been on the road most of your life. The sun enters at last, illuminating your small, birdlike features. You look exhausted and I know you should leave and rest. Yet I become selfish, almost rapacious in your presence. I long to detain you. You're going to leave, and in my panic, I no longer know what I'm saying. My questions become hazy, and I barely hear your replies – your voice emerges from a kind a fog. I want the vagueness to go on forever, engulfing the two of us. There is a particular energy filling the room – a slow, enveloping vertigo. Have you noticed it too? It is something like eternity. It is hard for you to leave; it is infinitely hard for me to see you go.

Every time we meet may be the last time. I am aware there are some things we will never say to one other. Certain words will remain unspoken, certain actions unperformed. There are vestiges buried underneath our gestures – a silent, ancient skeleton, never to be awoken. I never had the strength to lay my hand upon yours, not after what happened in Warsaw. I could never do it, even when your hand lies so near mine, even when we shared the same stage, the same rooms so many times before. I could never touch you again. I'm scared of you falling apart. It is not because of your physical brittleness after the illness – your extreme thinness, your fragility. Rather, I am afraid that something more unsubstantial may break in you – like the string of a fiddle suddenly snapping. I am afraid of a particular note, a certain melody dying. It is the fear of a sudden silence, of destroying something which will not come back. You've been broken before. I feel that holding yourself together, presenting yourself to the world, appearing before an audience is almost more than you can take now. You've been so ill. There is always a remainder of pain in the way you carry yourself – a trace of something that was there once and is now gone. You used to be so beautiful.

I notice the particular sound you make when you laugh and abruptly stop, as if reminded of something unpleasant. It is new. You're covering your tracks. But maybe there is nothing to cover. You reveal yourself in these moments of dissimulation. You hide nothing. You become disappearance itself. It is hard to know. You nearly died once, and now you're alive – miraculously.

You're coming to see me. In the days preceding your visit I can think of nothing else. I tidy the studio. And when you're gone, I don't even bother to clear the table. I leave things as they were, as they are. Everything is perfect as it is. There are ashes on the table and crumbs on the linoleum floor and I go straight to bed because I love you.

Your Door

Lynne Sargent

Your door is out there,
hidden in a nook of a weathered mansion,
standing solitary in a field,
lovingly carved into the stone of a cave,

it is bordered with the wallpaper
of a birthday party you weren't invited to
as a child,
stained with the smoke
of a parent's angry, controlling words,

except now it smells like your favourite cookies
and feels like love at first sight

it is the door that opens
releasing you into the world
and the one welcoming you home again.

You run your hands over it
and it has every splinter you remember
from those golden moments:

skidding across the deck
to cannonball into a pool,

gripping a tree limb as you rotate all the way around,
flipping for applause,

that picnic bench sliding back and forth
across your lower thighs that night of your first
& first dozen kisses.

I promise
the blazing sun of time has not bleached the meaning from it,
and it will unlock under your fingertips
so much easier than your own secrets

you will need not worry about keys
for it will know you
and who you want to enter.

wind & weather have not worn it down,
and though life may have worn you
your spine can find the space and will to stand
taller, for its frame will always accommodate
all of you, will always
bring you home.

To The Ones Greyed By The Blue-Stringed Ventriloquist

Neethu Krishnan

Dearest,

It is sneaky that way. Depression. You don't even notice it winding its indigo strings around your wrists.

Huh, this tightness is new, you think, but don't pause longer to dwell, *it is likely the new job, the relationship, the weather*, you comfort yourself.

The strings – all signature indigo – snake around your arms, your feet, your chest, stealthily, only tightening its coil at the unassuming soft of your neck. The sudden crush of it so choking, your eyes seem to lose relay with your rational mind, either flooding without cause or reason or parching so painfully dry, you ponder if you've always been this emotionally volatile.

Nothing makes sense.

Who doesn't have problems, a little sadness here and there, a shadowy existential crisis on and off? You chide yourself, starting to get frustrated at the laziness, the procrastination, the sense of hopelessness even when everything is seemingly alright, the leaden weight of your shortcomings only exponentiating with every sleepless night, the pythoning of the blue, once strings, now coir ropes.

You lament the once-rainbow-glow thoughts and glitter imprints, the attic of yesterdays having amassed an infinite supply of greys, pastels gone murky, and the glitter, now the soft glimmer of road asphalt. But all that's left of you is a pulp of unflattering, mottled greys.

Nothing's wrong, obviously; nothing serious anyway, becomes your new mantra.

There are so many in the world worse off than you, with real, tangible problems, you warn the quicksand darkness part of you.

You are not without grit, resilience, or the ability to positive-think your way to a less aphotic zone. The fantasy: to sleep and never rise; its wakeless continuum becomes a comforting sanctuary, its frigid jaws swallowing you into its icicle forest.

But you don't realize there's always an annoying somebody – a friend, like me, a stranger perhaps, a parent, a partner, a sibling, a classmate, a teacher, or even an impersonal internet search engine – who can see the indigo mummifying you. We can't help but notice the stray, concerning strings of night blue in errant, informal gestures or sentences, we see the yawning chasm where once there was a bridge to you.

You are defiant, in control, not broken or too broken to be fixed, but badgered by one of the above, you succumb. Reluctantly.

You let the sun, the pills, the couch, the vitamins, the friends, the solitude, the sweat, the white coats, the adventure, the retreat, the switch, the schedule, the greens, the books, the colours, the music sponge your hopelessness and darkness. Let it switch your indigo threads with shimmering golds and silvers one at a time.

After what seems like a lifetime and a quarter later, the silence becomes palpable, punctuated only with chirping squirrels, wind-tickled trees and your faint, rhythmic heartbeat.

Untethered, you will roam the ruins, marvelling at the world you once drowned out, cooing praises of salvation. You will remember you are light, not of a candle flame at the mercy of a draft, but the sterling silver of the moon and the warm gold of the sun that can only be clouded, never extinguished.

Self-Love

Tom Mallouk

Sometimes breaking down
is the beginning of breaking out
and you are free so slowly

and unevenly to learn self-love
the way brushing your teeth is an act
of self-love or buckling your seatbelt

or eating well, and especially ripe fruit,
how it bathes your tongue and suffuses
your mouth with sweetness, cleansing

the pasty taste of the shame you've carried.
Who knows why the dancer questions
her grace, the beautiful woman sees

only thickness in her thighs or the star
high school athlete imagines the world
a better place without him? No wonder,

it's daunting this notion of self-love.
But there is no mistaking the pleasure
of the fig when you finally wrest

your attention away from your failures:
bite into it, savor it, allow it to nourish you,
call it self-love.

With all the news for what ensues, I choose to hope and believe.

Jordan Zuniga

My dear friend,

There is much peril and sorrow within the world, with that there is no questioning or denying. The storms of life leaving hearts downcast and contrite over the calamities of yesterday just heard of in the news today, broadcasting the doom and gloom of all the wretched evils that take place in the world, and the depression that can be caused by the hopelessness of it all. The anxieties and fears of what lingers in the dark, either in the shadow of night or the uncertainties of tomorrow. The temptation to cry in despair and retreat. The news of loss of those we loved, and the painful sting of death that takes what is precious to us. The many different problems within the world and our inability to find solutions towards them all with any immediate success can feel overwhelming.

Yet with so much that goes on in the world and all the emotions tied to each and every thought, how often do we neglect our own health and wellbeing? To take care of our emotions and nurture our hearts to recognize that we are not without hope.

My dear friend, it should not be so! Though the days may seem dark under the downpour of the rain, all it means is that the sunshine will be clearer at the breaking of the gloomy veil. The night itself is a testament that though weeping may endure through the night, that God himself is faithful to bring the joy that comes in the morning. Our health need not be on the whims of opinions on urgent topics on the news alongside the speculation for what could be or what should be, but can be firmly protected by the renewing of our minds with the truth of all of it being worked by God himself for our good, and for God's glory, even if we don't necessarily perceive it as such. Take care, pray persistently, love deeply and tenderly, and never give up. We are called to run a race in life. So keep running no matter the storms and trials that be.

With love and encouragement,
-Your dear friend.

The Sky and the Sky and the Sky

Steve Denehan

My younger self would be surprised
would shake his head
at how
I can be happy
when I creak now
getting out of a chair
when I am breathless now
having run
to answer the phone
when I wake up stiff now
from sleeping
incorrectly

my younger self had nothing
left to learn
cocksure, smug
he knew it all and he would laugh
at this old dog
who, late in the game
has found that joy
is not in the knowing
but the learning

my younger self would not believe
the warmth of her small hand
the fine hairs on her arms
the melody that thrums
right through her centre
her fluttering butterfly lashes
cartwheeling soul and my heart
my thundering heart
as away she runs
on the balls of her feet
into the summertime breeze
and the musical trees
and the sky and the sky and the sky
and it is hers
every single bit of it is hers

The Sweetest Tough Cookie

For Alex Hart

B. Anne Adriaens

Keep a fox-in-a-box, every bone cleaned and accounted for,
and show it to the kids in your care—your punk roots compel you
to tell them there's more to their lives than what they are taught.

DJ at night, your tracks make a sound-grove for us who don't fit,
the forest sprites who mix the industrial with old woodlands
until the consensual paradox disappears.

DIY surrogate mother, you fight for the daughter
who's not officially yours, and are proof that punk is not dead
since you still battle for a less fucked-up future.

And when we meet at Mother's watering hole, that shrine
to the 80s we feel at home in, we can't complain as she pours
the best pint of Doombar and we play the longest game of pool.

To Braid a Cable

Chloe Orrock

There's this spider room in London Zoo
where they dangle and hang everywhere
like fanged nuts. The man there tells us
that if we made a cable from the thread
it could stop a jet pulling into the sky.
I think of the gossamer thinness
of a text or a birthday card; the gentle
strengthening of Sunday roasts and day trips;
the frantic spinning of reinforcements
when something punches a hole through the fabric
of the universe, which happens more these days
as we move into that age where more people
are grief-stricken than not. Hours on the phone,
a neck cricking on a sofa, gifting
not-alone-ness. We weave in the heat
of the reptile house, the poorly-timed rain,
the laughter of this baby who may be
a vanguard, ushering us to braid and braid.

Odysseus Wants To Hear About My School Play

Rachel Bruce

In my Year 8 class we performed the Odyssey.
I was a mariner, disposable.
My best friend wore your name.

Cunning were his ways too, and unfeeling.
He drew me in like a cyclone.
You would have liked him, I think;
his eyes were as sharp as yours.

We grew up in between lessons,
nursing each other out of childhood.
The summers were golden, coated in honey
and the wet tread of grass underfoot.
I admit I was I jealous of his gifts —
I felt mine were just as bright.
Still, it was a little miracle to be loved by someone.

The history of Troy pressed into the lawn
in the indents of folding chairs.
There we were enacting your trials,
children playing at immortality.

He was cruel to me —
though all of us are cruel in some way at that age.
I poured myself into him. He offered less in return.
I did not know then that I longed for him.
It is a difficult truth to learn,
that you love someone you cannot have.

I always wished I had been Circe;
so delicious to be the witch.
With the weight of my voice I would have called your myth to life.
Perhaps he would have liked it.

How all-consuming is teenage friendship;
every failure wounds deeply.
Still, I do not forgive everything —
it was not all forgivable.

I remember how he looked then,
his blue tunic shocking against the trees.
Your faces merge when I think of you.
He is what you look like to me.

We have not spoken in years.
Every year I remember his birthday less clearly.
The truth is we were but islands on the others' *nostos*.
We are both still floating between sands.

I suppose I was a little too in love with him.
I hate to think, Odysseus, that despite your flaws
I may have been a little in love with you too.

This Grimoire Belongs to Miss Cleo Jackson

Elis Montgomery

This Grimoire Belongs to: MiSS Cleo JAcKson

—

DEAR GRIMOR
Mom said I had magic appatood for frend making. I did it so fast and good. She said a witch rites it down. I am a witch. Billie is not a witch but maybe. She is not scared when I say poshuns.

Resipy for poshun frend making. Will work best on Billie.

Here you need
- apple joos box 6
- feather from the park where you met Billie
- the fluffy stuff like cloud on ground (dad said is a tree seed but looks like not)
- gravel from playgron where you did the zip with Billie and fell and cry
- a litle paint

To do making
1. Get the stuf
2. Get caldron
3. Put stuf in caldron

5. Ask mom for spoon
6. Stir it up
7. Put fingr in
8. Find wall
9. Fingr paint you and Billie on wall
10. You did it

The poshun works cus TODAY I ask Billie to be my best frend. Billie said yes.

—

SCIENCE EXPERIMENT by Cleo Age 9

Question: Was the potion I made in kindergarten real magic?

Hypothesis: Billie will be my friend no matter what because of the potion.

Procedure: Stop talking to Billie for 1 week.

Results: Billie is MAD!!!

Conclusion: I need to make a new potion.

Acknowledgements: Thank you Mom for teaching me the magic flame so I can make the potion again and keep it cooking forever.

New ingredients:
- acorn hats!!!
- purple sparkle crown Billie made for your birthday
- 2 bluebells like Billie's eyes
- eyelash from when you were rubbing your eyes, and Billie said make a wish, and you wished that Mom and Dad would be okay

Also potion is now tittled: THE FOREVER POTION OF FRIENDSHIP

—

Mom keeps bugging me to open this up again, like she thinks it'll help me cope or something. I guess no one told her she doesn't get to have opinions. Basically, I opened this but not because she said, and I'm only writing in here as a joke. But I've added stuff, so whatever.
- 1 Converse shoe charm necklace that says "Best"
- 2 tubes of lipstick stolen from your mother, cleansed under the light of a full moon
- ashes of the Ancient Rome partner paper of doom
- 1 tuft of stuffing from the bear Billie gave you when the divorce was finally a thing

And the steps are kind of important so here.
1. Light a candle, bone white as Billie's closet AKA the backdrop for your music videos
2. Meditate on how you'll die before anyone EVER sees the music videos
3. Slowly add the new ingredients to the cauldron, stir like it's a competition
4. After it's steeped awhile, take your "Best" necklace out and wear it so you still match her "Friend"
5. Ladle some potion into a heart flask from Urban Outfitters and keep it close (obviously don't drink it)
6. When people ask what's in the flask, pretend you're 17 and look chill

—

!!! important update
ingredients
- her acceptance letter to literal Cambridge
- she did not tell you she was applying to literal Cambridge
- what the fuck are you going to do without your best friend who's halfway across the world in literal Cambridge

instructions
1. pray?

—

Grimoire – excuse my absence. Blame forty overlong reading lists and probably that many parties (the novelty wore off by second year). The new recipe includes:
- 1 tbsp. pencil shavings
- 10 pkg. instant noodles
- 1 exorbitant phone bill from when you thought you were calling on Wi-Fi
- 1 chocolate hedgehog from the box Billie sent you in advance of Dad's nuptials
- roundtrip plane tickets
- polaroid of you, Billie, and her roommate Mia on the London Eye

Not all the lessons I'm learning revolve around ornithology. A selection:
1. Little me was right: a spelled flame can keep going forever but you have to tend to it. If the flicker dulls,

perform time zone math, and schedule a call with your best friend.

2. Sometimes the scent will change. The potion will evolve, need different things, and you'll have to adapt. Turns out your twenties are all about adapting.

3. Under NO circumstances shall you add tequila to the potion. At some point you're going to think it's a great idea and I'll tell you right now you're going to be wrong.

—

A Three-Step Guide to Potion-Making on Your Best Friend's Big Day

Step One: Immerse a set of plane tickets along with your invitation to the wedding of Billie Iverson and Mia Kim, already damp with happy tears.

Step Two: Instill one drop of the lemon-lavender perfume you gave Billie, spritzed above the high collar of her powder blue gown before she walked down the aisle.

Step Three: Douse 1 Hobnob, Mia's favourite, because you just got a best-friend-in-law.

—

Dearest Grimoire, an update.
Please add:
- 1 tiny UK flag, to thank England for giving Billie back, and lending Mia
- 1 pistachio macaron, from the baby shower that made you forget your every fear about turning thirty
- 1 tsp. tears, from when they told you what his name would be

This Grimoire Belongs to Miss Cleo Jackson Elis Montgomery

- 1 tag from "The Godson" onesie you got little Theo

And simmer so softly.

—

Grimoire: I'm learning how much love a heart can hold. In addition to a preservative herbal mixture, please infuse the following.
- Billie's letter, in all capitals, after you told her about Lucas, gentleman caller
- 2 tbsp. sparkling cranberry juice, from the picnic during which he secured Billie and Mia's approval, back in your park
- purple sparkle crown Billie made you when you got tenure
- 1 red ribbon, from your surprise 40th, with all those beaming faces (how is Theo this big already?)

As you brew, light your oil burner, and warm the amber resin Billie gifted you, calling it a "household deodorizer". Inhale the scents you, in your witch-hood, know foster love and luck.

—

A Floriography by Miss Cleo Jackson, Sage
- Peony *(promise)* — for your godson's engagement
- Orchid *(beauty)* — for his wife, glowing
- Rosemary *(remembrance)* — for their angel baby
- Magnolia *(long-awaited joy)* — for their rainbow baby
- Yellow poppies *(congratulations)* — for Billie and

Mia, calling each other "Grandma" in the delivery room
and touching tiny baby girl toes
Add a petal of each, to fortify.

—

A Senior Witch's Tips for the Best Brew
    1.   Age, if you've been blessed with the option. Keep the potion cooking. Sometimes you'll need to turn the heat down, let it bubble gently in the background while you tend to more pressing tinctures, like the one for your grief, and hers.* Your health, and hers.**
    2.   Always keep the recipe. If not in a grimoire, then in the hollowed-out book you stuffed with doodles from math class; birthday cards with no white space left; missives written in cursive, because you can't clutch a holo-message to your chest.
    3.   Don't have children and grandchildren or do. You'll pass on the recipe either way. It's been cooking all these years; the people around you can't help but smell it. Share in moderation. Always keep enough for yourself.
*add rosemary for remembrance once more, a sprig for each of your parents
**add borage oil, for your joints; add lavender, for her relaxation once treatment starts

—

Add magnolia, for Theo's second rainbow baby, and her Billie-blue eyes.

—

Add the lilies Billie gave you when you interred Lucas's ashes. Add a bookmark, to hold your place.

—

Ingredients
- 1 Hobnob, Mia's favourite, to say goodbye
- The casserole leftovers you can't get Billie to eat
- Black cottonwood seed, from the first walk you got her to go on, after
- Mint leaves from your garden, because you can only brew her so much tea

Instructions
1. Do what you can

—

When Theo gives you Billie's "Friend" charm, see that it's just as tarnished as your "Best." Cradle both necklaces in a weathered palm. Realize you can't tell where one bronzed chain ends and the other begins.

Add them to the cauldron, unpolished. Let them be evidence of what you've weathered together.

—

Still keep it brewing. You have to keep the flame alive. If nothing else, the potion can last.

—

Grimoire, every time I catch sight of you, it's a revelation. You're still here. You're in the bookshelf, on my desk, tucked into the couch cushions. But there's no mischievous brownie to blame for moving you around. It's me. I've been leaving you places. I pick you up, intending to write. But then.

We held the celebration of life in her garden, all of us wearing her blue. The grandchildren toddled by the foxgloves during the readings. Afterwards, Theo led me up to Billie's study.

To see her cauldron.

She must've had a travel version stuffed somewhere because there was no way you were getting that thing on a plane. Larger than mine, even. Cast iron. The fire had gone out, of course, but when you stoke a spelled flame that long, it goes slow.

Steam still wafted up. I leaned in and felt the lingering warmth. Smelled the apple juice, the lemon-lavender, the mint.

I lowered my palm to Billie's own potion of everlasting friendship. Warm as the milk you'd give a baby. Behind me, Theo graciously withdrew.

These old bones got down on the floor to sit by the cauldron. To spend a little more time with you, Billie.

Ingredients
- Speeches from a dozen dear friends and a son that would've brought you the moon
- Poems that rhyme "Bubbe" with "love you",

tripping out of the mouths of grandchildren
- A thousand hugs, more smiles
- The letters. Oh, the letters
- The luck I had to find you so early in life, and to keep you so long
- The blessing that was you tending to it too, always
- Maybe one more feather, one left by a nighthawk in a park where two little girls met

Instructions
1. Find a friend who will love you back just as fiercely
2. Hold on tight

Not Half Jar of Peanut Butter

Colette Tennant

But some things are prettier in halves –
grapefruits for instance,
spokes of a sweet, sour wheel.
A hard-boiled egg,
one meaty sun in the midst
of all that white.
And two halves of a concord grape,
they shine beyond hyphenation.
And the waxing moon, demure,
so it hides half its pretty face.
And open books –
even and odd in either hand,
and high tea for two, equilateral friendship
in geometries of bread,
and a folded pillow, lifting your face
a little closer to the stars.

A letter to a friend about scrambled eggs

Jon Chan

July, 1902

My friend,

I have not gone native. Nor have I betrayed the ideals of our Homeland and I remain loyal to the Emperor. But my experiences here in London cannot be ignored.

Today, virtue presented itself to me, in this piss-soaked, opium-addled place. They called it scrambled eggs — it is a revelation. Yes, we have scrambled eggs back home. My friend, I still remember eating Whampoa stir-fried eggs with shrimp overlooking the bay in Kowloon. However, these eggs reveal a different philosophy.

The chef permitted me to watch. The demonstration reminded me of watching people practicing qigong in the square. It began with a flat pan over a low heat. I have often dismissed the flat pan because it does not allow for the concentration of breath, and I suspect this is why the cuisine of the British is so often mushy.

But I digress. The eggs are cracked, and the contents of the shells are dumped whole into the pan along with what I can only describe as a fist of butter. No whisking. No salt. No sugar. Not even a pinch of starch. Then with a wooden spoon, the chef stirred the mixture. And stirred. And stirred. For at least two marks, he stirred the mixture as it slowly solidified.

I must say, at first, it appeared less than appetizing. The

substance the chef scraped out of the pan looked like yellow silk tofu. In this snot-like state, the chef added seasoning, consisting of only salt and black (not white) pepper.

The eggs were served with twice-baked bread, charred tomato, sausage, and cooked pig's blood.

Most of what I ate confirmed what I believe about the efficacy of the frying pan. However, the eggs were the one exception. They were moist without being oily and soft without being slimy. My friend, you probably want news about the treaty and not about eggs. The only detail I can pass along is that — this is the first time in living memory that we are *writing* as well as *signing* policy.

What I am really trying to say is this: I cannot learn without acknowledging my own ignorance. Up until yesterday, I believed there was only one way to make scrambled eggs. And today, I have opened my mind to another. Perhaps you think it trivial. However, I assure you that I have thought about this a great deal. The scrambled eggs lead back to a different technique, which leads back to a different type of tool, to a different type of stove, and culminates to a whole other school of cooking. I am also hopeful because the chef has given me a chance to show him our methods for scrambled eggs. That is next week. Today, I am to be shown a new culinary invention, and I hope it is good. They call it *Marmite*.

Spaghetti Bridge

Izzy Searle

Do you remember when we built bridges from spaghetti that shattered as soon as Miss put an egg on it? Yeah, Jess Drayton's team won instead. No, I haven't seen her since, have you?

Who else do you still talk to? How is he? No, I messaged the maths lot a bit but they – hey, do you remember when we built bridges from spaghetti? Yeah, what a mess! And when we moved our desk one inch to the right each time Sir turned his back to write on the board. No, don't pin this on me, that was your idea! I was trying to pay –

so what do you do now? Wow, ok. No, I just always pictured something different for you. Like a park ranger or something? Or a gardener then, I don't know! No, I haven't painted in a long time, gave all that up when I – do you remember when we built bridges from – no, I know I was good, but there's no money in it, not for newcomers. Well my landlord wasn't going to wait until I was famous to charge – bridges from spaghetti, you remember?

Or when we hid behind a tree to get out of PE? No, that was a different time, but that was funny too. A different time. Just think, we used to bunk PE, but now I pay £180 a year to go to the gym.

Do you remember when we used to build – how's your Mum? Sorry to hear that. Bridges from spaghetti?

You know, my daughter came home the other day saying they use marshmallows now to stick the spaghetti – yeah, I have two, do you have kids? Do you want any?

Do you remember when we used to stay late in DT sanding down our bird boxes. Mum's still got mine in the garden.

>Different times.

If you could go back and do it all again, would you? Really? Well I would, I guess. You and me sat back in the school field, copying each other's answers before class, chatting about who's dating who – you know Mia and Holly are still together? – unwrapping melting chocolate bars, rolling up our sleeves to get a tan, spaghetti in our school bags for later, not worrying about schedules or fitting each other in because we'd see each other tomorrow and the tomorrow after that and the –

>do you remember when we built bridges from spaghetti?

Will Oceans Converge in Our Village Park?

Alex Harford

We leave my parents' house in our wetsuits, hiking the grassy slopes into the valley and past the abandoned bungalows we used to live in. At the old playground, we take turns pushing the roundabout while the other sits, eyes closed to the stinging rain and dizziness.

Puddles form into a pond, and when it's my turn to ride, I dip my toes as we spin, creating feet-high foot-tsunamis around the base of the roundabout.

As it slows, you glance up to the iron-grey clouds and crackling thunder. "When can we call this biblical?"

"When the park becomes an ocean?" I reply.

Since my parents' boat capsized, I hadn't been near a lake, never mind an ocean. I couldn't leave the shallow end of the swimming pool. My heart would pound as I struggled to keep my head up, tasting the chlorine-bleached water.

"Would you be scared? If you remembered how you nearly drowned?" I ask.

"If I saw it happen to you yes, but I know you're a good swimmer."

Was.

Pushing becomes a slog, so we wade, shin-deep, to the two swings.

You stand, holding the faded red-to-pink seat. "First to push the swing over five times wins."

Throwing the swings over the bar *would* shorten the

chains for when we sit, allowing more room for our legs to build momentum.

But the darkening sky sends shivers like cold lightning up my spine. "How much deeper will it get?"

You smile and place a hand on my shoulder. I was glad you were spending your last day in the country with me.

"Remember when we tried to swing over the bars?" I say.

"We got nowhere near."

This time, we push and throw the swings over the bar. Yours plonks onto your head. We laugh so hard my sides ache. Wind wraps my wet hair around my face, and the water deepens as fast as I can push the swing over. Yours is four times around and mine two.

"Nice one," I say, out of breath.

You dare us to swing as high as we can. We sit and swing – sending canoe-oar ripples with our toes and powerboat wakes with our ankles – as the water rises and rises.

When the water reaches our knees, we lose our momentum.

"When does a pond become a lake?" you ask.

Water laps over my thighs. "No idea, but the wind's making waves now. How deep is it?"

You stand and sway, the waves neck high. We should have left, but I promised we'd spend the day together where we first met. Despite our wetsuits, I hadn't thought the valley would flood.

I was a little scared lightning would strike us, but the slide was the highest thing in the park. Higher than the basketball hoop and the top of the swings, higher than the old bungalows.

"Let's swim."

You knew where to. "Race you!"

I jump from the swing and stumble. Earthy water sloshes into my mouth. Your hands on my shoulders, you steady me.

"Three, two, one, go!" I shout.

You swim backstroke, and I swim breaststroke. Anxious to escape the water, I beat you by a head. You climb the slide's ladder and hold your arms aloft.

"I didn't say to the top." I laugh, climb up, and push you down the slide. You go head-first – *splash*. I follow – *splash*. For a second, I forget my fear, but with my head above water I can only touch the ground on my toes, which sink into the mud. My chest tightens. I swim around to the ladder and thrash at the handles.

We climb back to the top and huddle between the metal rails, your warmth seeping into me through our wetsuits. Lightning flashes, and thunder claps. The rain becomes heavier, and the water rises further.

You point to two toy figures washing by, face up. "You forgot how easy it is to float."

"Maybe."

The figures drift together and apart, together and apart. Until they are too far away to see.

Dusk comes early, with no sign of sun. We watch the world disappear around us. Streetlamps flicker overhead. The water glints as it rises over our toes.

"When does a lake become an ocean?" you say.

"When the deepest parts can't be reached by light?"

The streetlamps die completely. A biting wind blows from the north, and we can't huddle any closer. But I don't want to leave.

When the storm clears enough to reveal glimmering lights up in the villages, I say, "We should go."

We sit for a few minutes, maybe an hour more. In silence. Feeling each other's heartbeats and breath. Rubbing each other's pruned hands for warmth.

I squeeze your hand. "We really should go."

"I'll come with you."

Our houses are on opposite sides.

"You can't swim to one side and all the way back to the other." I was more concerned about letting *you* leave on your own than I was about swimming myself.

"I don't want to go," you say.

I gulp and wipe a tear away. It probably looked like rain. "Neither do I. But we have to."

It was becoming colder, and we hadn't eaten since breakfast. We climb down the two yet-to-be-submerged ladder steps, prolonging every second we can. We tread water, warming our bodies. You hold my hand while I float on my back, drifting away from the safety of the slide.

You let go, but my pulse races and I sink.

You squeeze my hand, and I relax. It is easy, like you said. We caress each other's cheeks with our fingertips, and then we swim apart.

By the time I get home, the rain has stopped. I sit under a warm quilt, holding a hot chocolate I'm too worried to sip. I watch through my bedroom window and wait for your signal. I pray the clouds won't drop again.

Three flashes of a torch, for our three years together.

I flash my torch in return.

10 Names of Happiness

A poetic description of ten words for happiness in the Arabic language

Taher Adel

فَرَح

the inverse of sadness
(pronounced: Farah)

This happiness does not see eye to eye
with sadness, it does not know its name
it does not recognise the scars that paved the road
but it walks it all the same.

نَعِيم

the source of comfort
(pronounced: Na'eem)

This happiness trickles forth from its source
like a hot spring, it finds my body cold
and warms every inch of me
heart, to flesh, to bones
until I am a sponge amongst stone.

سُرور
A moment of contentment in the heart
(pronounced: Suroor)

You enter my heart
and your touch grinds
time to a halt
I live in this moment
as if secured with lock and bolt
and that moment is inconceivably full,
full to the brim with you.

غِبْطَة
blessedness
(pronounced: Ghibta)

This happiness is nothing short of divine
every pull of sadness is fought with a smile.

بَشَاشَة
happiness to the point of laughter
(pronounced: Bashasha)

This is happiness that bypasses woe
until it erupts as laughter
the lava of happiness melting
every layer of your hard exterior.

هَنَاء

To live in bliss
(*pronounced: Hana'a*)

If happiness was a person
it would have your face
because to live with you
is to live in bliss.

بَهْجَة

the vivid expression of joy
(*pronounced: Bahja*)

My heart has entered spring
and my face is flowering
and every smile invites a bee
for a cup of nectar laced with seeds.

بِشْر

To rejoice
(*pronounced: Bishir*)

This is happiness that lives on in eyes
as infectious as the spread of your smile
every moment here is a celebration
and celebrations like you
light up the night.

نَشْوَة

Intoxicated by happiness
(pronounced: Nashwa)

This happiness is a sugar rush
maybe a little too much?
Too sweet for an untrained tongue
Will sadness now become
my hangover?

سَعَادَة

To rise in happiness
(pronounced: Sa'ada)

To ascend beyond clouds,
beyond our sphere of despair
a kite battling wind, lungs battling air
until I'm faced with nothing
but your radiant smile and
sun, sun everywhere.

Author biographies

Alex Harford is a writer and photographer from Staffordshire. He loves visiting places that don't seem real, being outdoors, music, 90s video games, and film. Alex doesn't enjoy bacon and/or cake as much as some people think and has a website at https://AlexHarford.uk

Angela Townsend is the development director at a cat sanctuary. She graduated from Princeton Seminary and Vassar College. Her work appears or is forthcoming in *Arts & Letters, Paris Lit Up, Pleiades, SmokeLong Quarterly,* and *Terrain,* among others. Angie has had Type 1 diabetes for 34 years.

B. Anne Adriaens is a Belgian immigrant based in Somerset. Her work has appeared in various magazines and anthologies, including *Poetry Ireland Review, Ink Sweat and Tears, Emerge Literary Journal, Skylight 47, The Other Side of Hope, Abridged, Acumen, Amsterdam Quarterly* and *Stand Magazine* (forthcoming).

Briony Collins has three books with Broken Sleep Books – *Blame it on Me, All That Glisters,* and *The Birds, The Rabbits, The Trees* – as well as *Whisper Network* (Bangor University) and *cactus land* (Atomic Bohemian). She has three books forthcoming in 2025, including her debut novel with Barnard Publishing.

Chloe McIntosh (she/her) is a poet living in Hertfordshire. She has a BA in English Literature from the University of Exeter and was shortlisted for the Platypus Press Celestial Bodies Poetry Prize while studying there. Her work has appeared or is forthcoming in *Briefly Write, Utopia Science Fiction, WayWords* and elsewhere. You can find her on instagram at @chloemcintoshwriter

Chloe Orrock (she/they) is a writer and actor from the Midlands (UK), based in London. Her poetry has featured recently in journals including *Púca, Skylight 47, RockPaperPoem,* and *ChannelMag,* and she won the Sentinel Literary Quarterly Prize. She is interested in ritual, grief, and transformation. Twitter: @ChloeOrrock but she mainly tweets about snooker.

Colette Tennant has three books of poetry: *Commotion of Wings, Eden and After,* and *Sweet Gothic,* just published. Her book, *Religion in The Handmaid's Tale: a Brief Guide,* was published in 2019 to coincide with Atwood's publication of *The Testaments.* Her poems have won various awards and have been nominated for Pushcart Prizes.

Daisy Edwards (she/her) is an autistic, bisexual writer living in Birmingham with her husband and cat. Her poetry has been featured in *Written Off's Ey Up 2*, *Spelt Magazine*, and the *York Literary Review*, among other brilliant indie presses. Follow her on Instagram @dredwards_writes

Elis Montgomery is a speculative fiction writer from Vancouver, Canada. She is a member of SFWA and Codex. When she's not writing, she's usually hanging upside down in an aerial arts class or a murky cave. Find her there or at elismontgomery.com.

Ell Huang (she/they) is an aroace writer of fantasy, horror, and platonic love. She reads for *Whale Road Review* and is published in 130+ venues such as *Moss Puppy*, *Lumiere Review*, *miniskirt magazine*, *Tealight Press*, *Not Deer Magazine*, *Quail Bell*, *Resurrection Mag*, and more. They're currently writing *Aromantic Frankenstein*.

Ella Sadie Guthrie is a writer who often fails at being funny. She is the co-host of Words By The Water in Brighton and co-founded WRIOT, a poetry collective for womxn and non-binary poets. Her first pamphlet *Poems For Pete Davidson* was published by Broken Sleep Books in 2022. Her first full collection *Scorpio Szn* is out with Write Bloody UK. She splits her time between Athens and Brighton, but you can mostly find her daydreaming.

Elodie A. Roy is a French-born writer living in Newcastle upon Tyne, England. Her fiction appears in *The Stinging Fly*, *3:AM Magazine*, *Flash Frog*, *New World Writing*, *Bending Genres*, and elsewhere. Elodie has recently won a Faber Academy scholarship and is currently working on her debut novel. Contact: e.a.roy@riseup.net

Izzy Searle is an award-winning writer from Sussex. Her poetry has been published by *Streetcake*, *Blue Marble Review*, *Olney Magazine*, and more. Her play, *Baggy Bra*, won Best Comedy Play at the Greater Manchester Fringe. She is @izzysearlewriter on Instagram and LinkedIn, and her website is www.izzysearlewriter.com.

Jane Burn is an award-winning hybrid writer and working-class person with autism / person with a disability. Her current collection, *Be Feared*, is available from Nine Arches. Her next collection, *The Apothecary of Flight*, will be published in July, also by Nine Arches. She is the Michael Marks Awards Environmental Poet of the Year 2023/24.

Jon Chan is a writer of all sorts. Works that he has published cover everything from intergalactic war to how to make scrambled eggs. When he's not writing, he enjoys exploring all over his native New England. He demands that you have a nice day!

Jordan Zuniga is a Christian and conservative poet, devotional, and creative writer who enjoys honoring his Lord and Savior with His creativity. He has appearances with *Creation Illustrated*, the *Lorelei Signal*, and others. Readers and inquiring literary agents who are interested in offering representation and/or supporting his creativity can follow and contact him on Instagram @cccreativewriter.

Lynne Sargent is a writer, aerialist, and holds a Ph.D in Applied Philosophy. They are the poetry editor at *Utopia Science Fiction magazine*. Their work has been nominated for Rhysling, Elgin, and Aurora Awards, and has appeared in venues such as *Augur Magazine, Strange Horizons*, and *Daily Science Fiction*. To find out more visit them at scribbledshadows.wordpress.com.

Mabel Ros was born in Spain, where she studied arts, design and animation and moved to the United Kingdom when she was 22. She learned English and graduated with a degree in art history and creative writing and is now merging her art and writing worlds. Ros lives in South Wales with her cat Gandalf.

Maggie D'Isa-Hogan is a California-based writer and undergraduate. She writes satirical articles for both *The Hard Times* and *Hard-Drive.net*. Her creative non-fiction can be read in publications such as *Mslexia Literary Magazine* and *Ruby Magazine*. She can be found on instagram: @maggie_disa

Melissa Joplin Higley is the author of *First Father* (Bottlecap Press). Her poems appear in *B_O_D_Y, Feral, Sleet Magazine, Whale Road Review, Writer's Digest*, and elsewhere. She holds an MFA from Sarah Lawrence College, co-founded and co-facilitates the Poetry Craft Collective, and co-edits book reviews for *MER*. Visit her online: melissajoplinhigley.com

Marie Vibbert's short fiction has appeared in top magazines like *Nature, Analog*, and *Clarkesworld*, and been translated into Czech, Chinese and Vietnamese. She was a 2023 Hugo and Nebula nominee for her novelette, *We Built This City*. She also writes poetry, comics, and computer games. By day she is a computer programmer in Cleveland, Ohio.

Neethu Krishnan is a writer based in Mumbai, India. A Best of the Net Poetry nominee and Bacopa Literary Review Creative Nonfiction Award winner, she was also longlisted for the 2024 Erbacce Poetry Prize. Her works have been curated in 30+ international publications so far.

Olivia Walwyn's poetry has been published in a range of magazines and anthologies; most recently *Spelt, Acumen* and *Alba*. She has a pamphlet, *En Route*, and collection, *Halcyon*, published by Templar. She lives in Norwich where she works as a Library and Information Assistant.

Rachel Bruce (she/her) is a poet based in South London. Her work has appeared in *The Poetry Review*, *Propel Magazine*, *Mslexia*, *Ink Sweat and Tears*, *The Telegraph*, and *Atrium*, among others.

Sarah Terkaoui is an Irish/Syrian poet. She was shortlisted for the Cinnamon Press Poetry Pamphlet Award 2022, commended for the Goldsmiths Poetry Festival and Hippocrates Poetry Prize 2021, and longlisted for the Live Canon international poetry Prize 2021. She is published in *Black Iris*, *Ink Sweat & Tears*, *Imposter*, *Porridge*, *Green Ink Poetry*, *Persimmon Review*, *Propel*, *The Storms*, *Visual Verse*, and *Dreich*. She has an MA in Writing Poetry (Newcastle University/ Poetry School London).

Sodïq Oyèkànmí is a poet, dramaturg and translator. A 2022/23 Poetry Translation Centre (UK) UNDERTOW Fellow. He is a recipient of the Unserious Collective Fellowship (2023) and won the Sevhage/ Hyginus Ekwuazi Poetry Prize (2023). His works appear in various literary journals and magazines. Twitter/X @sodiqoyekan

Steve Denehan lives in Kildare, Ireland with his wife Eimear and daughter Robin. He is the author of two chapbooks and five poetry collections. Winner of the Anthony Cronin Poetry Award and twice winner of Irish Times' New Irish Writing, his numerous publication credits include *Poetry Ireland Review* and *Westerly*.

Taher Adel, a British-Bahraini poet, holds an MA in Creative Writing from the University of East Anglia. He was a judge for the Stephen Spender Poetry Prize and Poet in Residence for Wells-next-the-Sea. His works appear in *Ambit*, *Poetry London*, *BBC Radio*, and *TedX*.

Tom Mallouk is a United States poet who has published two chapbooks: *Nantucket Revisited* in 2013 and *The Write Metaphor* in 2023. He is the emeritus poet laureate of Bucks County, Pennsylvania and the creator and curator of the Poet's Corner, a weekly poetry feature in the *Bucks County Herald*. www.tommallouk.org

Yana Fay Dzedze, is an interdisciplinary artist, and writer. She cradles and champions creativity and unhindered self-expression. English-German, and born to travelling parents, Yana's life has been steeped in cultural diversity from the moment she was born. Based between the UK and South Africa, Yana now lives with her Xhosa husband and their daughter. Her memoirs, *The Fire in My Belly*, and *You Came With the Birds* unpack the complexity of intercultural and interracial relationships through her own personal stories, with belonging as a key theme throughout.